# Hey Gang!

## Ready to Go-Go?

Carey Masci

Copyright © 2014 by Carey Masci

*Hey Gang! Ready to Go-Go?*

Carey Masci, author

Michael T. Petro, Jr., editor

PetroPublications.com

Published in the United States of America

ISBN-10: 1500678945

ISBN-13: 978-1500678944

# Dedication

Ever since I was just six weeks old, I've been traveling. That first trip, according to Dad, was in a '63 Buick station wagon, pulling a 12-foot Hi-Lo, filled with Dad, Mom, three kids and Uncle Joe. We were off to Cumberland, Kentucky. Needless to say, I don't remember much of those early trips.

Well, as soon as I was old enough to drive, off I went on my own, staying off the main highways and always traveling the back roads; in doing so, I have met the most interesting people and seen the most unique sights.

Another habit of mine is to shop at the little mom and pop shops and rarely do I eat fast food or at the corporate restaurant, but usually at the little diner or family restaurant. Some of the places look condemned from the outside, but seldom has a meal been disappointing.

I also have that knack for finding little towns with friendly people who have countless stories waiting to be told.

This book is dedicated to these people.

# Table of Contents

Preface.................................................…..…VIII

Introduction: Dad's Tire Tracks....................…...…......1

Chapter 1. Breakfast...............................…..….......4

Chapter 2. The Blessing of the Ships.............…...….....6

Chapter 3. A Scene from the Kentucky Trip............…...10

Chapter 4. Careyisms.............................….........13

Chapter 5. Beaver Creek, Buttermilk Falls and Fish...16

Chapter 6. Looking for Gators...........................21

Chapter 7. Notes from Boston...........................23

Chapter 8. The Spinning Spatula

　　　　　　　 – A Scene from the Manhattan Trip.........28

Chapter 9. The Dark Stranger of Summerville, Texas..31

Chapter 10. Nighttime Rainbow.........................35

Chapter 11. Short Trips..........................…........36

Chapter 12. The Car Trip.............................…..... 39

Chapter 13. The Toilet Incident.........................51

Chapter 14. I Love a Parade............................…..53

Chapter 15. Easter 2010..............................…....55

Chapter 16. New York City Traffic.....................60

Chapter 17. Clifton Gorge, Clifton Mill &

　　　　　　　 Yellow Springs, Ohio – Review 2013......63

Chapter 18. The Costly Resort...........................65

Chapter 19. My Review of the Pemberville Free Fair..67

Chapter 20. The Cleveland Submarine...................70

Chapter 21. Elk Viewing................................72

Chapter 22. The Wisconsin Dells Trip....................75

Chapter 23. Notes from Texas.............................83

Chapter 24. Anything to See...............................86

Chapter 25. The Factory of Terror.........................87

Chapter 26. That's Old......................................93

Chapter 27. Road to a Friend's House....................94

Chapter 28. Thank God for Teachers.....................97

Chapter 29. The Sandy Lake Supper.....................98

Chapter 30. A BANG........................................101

In Closing...................................................103

# Preface

## What is the premise of this book?

This book is travel-related, but not in the traditional sense. It's a light-hearted, fun look at the great American road trip by way of my amusing and entertaining travel experiences, adventures, misadventures, gaffes and many laughs. Some are written in story form, others are JUST notes and highlights.

## Why did I write this book?

I live quite a full life with many twists and turns, never knowing where my next invite may take me or what unique experience I may stumble upon.

I have been writing about these experiences for years via blogs, and sharing them with friends by sending countless emails. It was my family and friends who kept encouraging me to write a book...though I'm not certain if they really liked my writings or just wanted me to write a book, so I would quit sending emails.

## What was my inspiration?

America is a beautiful country with numerous natural and manmade sites to see but, really, it's the people who make this nation great. I am a "people person" and would rather sit and converse with someone over a cup of coffee than just about anything else. Like so many other things in America, the art of conversation is also in decline because of our fast-paced lifestyle and computerized way of communicating with short tweets and misspelled words. You need to slow down and make time for people.

Everyone has a story to tell; all you have to do is listen!

## Are all these stories true?

Yes, all these stories are true and the people mentioned are real. In the first draft of the book, I had the word "friend" written over and over to the point of redundancy. So, I rewrote it and, if the story really had little to do with who I was with, their names were omitted (sorry) but, if a friend or acquaintance is part or a focal point in the story, a name is included.

## Why should you buy this book?

It's a very easy read that gives you a break from all the serious, crazy things going on in our world today.

Besides, the fun-filled stories in this book also have a useful aspect. If you want to take notes of the places or sites mentioned, you could use it as a travel guide and visit them yourself.

Another reason is I need to pay off the publisher. If you don't buy this book, it comes out of my pocket, so buy the book and support a good cause of replenishing my pockets. I could also use the gas money for my next road trip. Anyone coming?

# Introduction

## Dad's Tire Tracks

Dad always loved travelling and road trips. He preferred the less-traveled roads and night travel. Our family vacations usually followed this pattern. While other families were going to amusement parks, we were on the back roads in search of some recreated pioneer or Indian village, shrine, or a large something, such as a button collection.

A couple of the "forgettable" memorable trips that I remember quite well were the trips to Big Muskie and the Blue Hole. Big Muskie was a behemoth dragline, used to unearth coal in southern Ohio. Dad was so excited to see this 22-story-tall machine with a bucket so large, it could hold two Greyhound buses. Dad even had Mom and us kids excited. We drove way out to the middle of nowhere on some twisty country road, and there it was – Big Muskie. The only problem was we couldn't get close to it. Big Muskie was so far off in the distance, it looked small. A bigger problem than not getting to see it arose when Dad had to turn the car around towing a 21-foot Fan trailer. I remember him yelling at mom, "GET THE KIDS OUT NOW AND GO." Dad told me years later that he thought, if the car went off the cliff, at least only he would have died.

Then there was the Blue Hole in Castalia. Dad took us to see this neat attraction at least twice. The Blue Hole was supposedly bottomless, its depth unknown. I remember after paying, walking through a rather long entrance to reach this perfectly round pond with a guardrail around it. That's all you got to see. How exciting! Well, it was thrilling for a young boy with an imagination, thinking about falling in and never reaching bottom.

Such fun-filled memories! Those family vacations and adventures never left me. Because of them, I've followed in Dad's tire tracks and carried on his passion for the open road, as I love to do the exact same thing: back-road travel, night travel, and looking for the obscure.

Besides traveling and enjoying the outdoors, I followed in Dad's tire tracks in another way. Dad's favorite vehicles were his '63 Buick Invicta station wagon and his bright orange '75 Ford Econoline van. I also went from wagons to vans, finally to the perfect travel vehicle: a 1969 Dodge Xplorer motor home I restored and nicknamed the Go-Go Bus.

The original title of the '69 Dodge has it listed as a house-car. Motor home, house car, Go-Go Bus, Lunar Module, Barney Mobile, New Age Mystery Machine, are just a few of the many names it's been called. But, whatever you call it, I am never alone when driving this two-tone purple people greeter; someone is always coming up to me to inquire about it.

The Go-Go Bus has actually taken on its own "retro" active travel identity. For instance, I was in the Maple Festival Parade in Chardon, Ohio. I took third place in the car division. The first and second place winners were listed by owner and the vehicle they drove but, for third place, all it said was "Third Place: Go-Go Bus." I was never mentioned.

Driving the Go-Go Bus has led to even more adventures and opportunities to meet people and receive invites of all kinds. In fact, it even inspired a website and this book, which highlights just some of the many travel experiences I've had with the Go-Go Bus and without.

So, grab your travel mug, sit back, and let's start the adventure...

# Chapter One

## Since this is the first chapter let's start with...

## Breakfast!

I am not sure exactly where I was on this particular road trip, but somewhere in Ohio, and I don't remember the restaurant we stopped at either, but I do remember the setting of the place and the overly-stern waitress that could make a hardboiled egg look soft.

A friend and I woke up late and were looking for breakfast. We stopped at a family restaurant. I ordered breakfast, but the waitress informed us that "It is after 11:00 a.m. - we are only serving lunch." I replied, "It's only a little bit after 11:00 a.m. and this is our first meal of the day. Can't I order just a couple of eggs with toast and hash browns?" "NOPE, you have to order from the lunch menu." "I'm really not into a big meal. You sure I can't order just a couple of eggs...nothing special, with toast and hash browns?" "I said YOU CAN'T. This is our lunchtime. Breakfast is over." And she wasn't pleasant explaining this either.

I said, "Well, if I can't order something as simple as eggs with toast, we are just going to leave, and forget my coffee." I was about to get up when she said, "Well, why don't you order an egg sandwich with a side of hash browns?" I asked, "What's an egg sandwich?" "It's two pieces of toast with an egg between it."

I just about fell on the floor laughing and asked, "What's the difference between two pieces of toast and two eggs with a side of hash browns or an egg sandwich and a side order of hash browns?" The loveable waitress said, "I TOLD YOU, one is breakfast and the other is lunch. NOW, DO YOU WANT IT OR NOT?"

I got the egg sandwich, but you know what? It still tasted like breakfast to me.

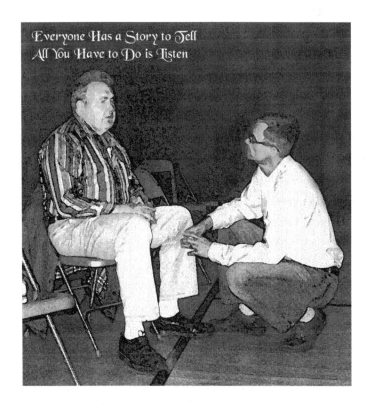

# Chapter Two

## The Blessing of the Ships

So many things I do, I just stumble upon. No planning - just walk right into them. For instance, I was asked if I could deliver a cabinet bought in Cleveland to an office in Ashtabula, Ohio. Of course I said "Yes."

The quickest way to Ashtabula from Cleveland is taking Rt. 90, the freeway, and exiting at Rt. 45, but I prefer Rt. 20. Rt. 20 is the old route that everyone drove before the advent of the freeway; it will take you all the way to the East Coast.

I picked up Rt. 20 in Painesville Township. The cities and towns you drive through from Painesville Twp. are Perry, Madison, Geneva, Saybrook and then, Ashtabula. The office was close to the Ashtabula Harbor. I found it with ease. After unloading the cabinet, I took a drive to see what's in the area.

I am not very familiar with Ashtabula, so can't tell you where I was at. I took a right at an intersection. On the side street before it, there was a church with police cars and a crowd of people in front. I spun around towards the church to investigate. It looked like maybe a wedding or a graduation, but why the cop cars?

At the stop sign in front of the church, I asked a lady what was going on. She said that they were going to bless the ships. What? I had to park and find out. I asked another lady, "What's going on?" "It's the blessing of the ships." OK, one more time. I'll ask this man; maybe he will tell me the full story. "Excuse me. What's going on?" "It's the blessing of the fleet. We are marching down to the harbor with the bishop and priest to pray for the ships' safety. The Father sprinkles water over them." I ask, "Is this something new?" "Nope! It's the 61$^{st}$." I guess I missed a few, huh?

I can't believe I forgot his name. Usually, I remember everything, so we'll just call him Mr. Cordial. Mr. Cordial said they were about set to march and I could join in. I ran to my van and grabbed my camera. What timing, and little did I know I'd parked on the parade route.

First in line were the Knights of Columbus 4$^{th}$ Degree Honor Guard, then the bagpipers, followed by Father Ruggieri, Bishop Murray of Youngstown, and walking behind were the congregation and friends of Mother of Sorrows Church.

I asked Mr. Cordial if he minded if I tagged alongside him. He said, "Absolutely not!" I had my own personal tour guide. As we walked, he told me the history of Ashtabula Harbor. At one time it was the third largest in the country, behind New York City and Long Beach in California. Ashtabula was a prime fishing area. There were many fisheries and charter services, private and commercial; charters still exist today, but nothing like its heyday before the fish were just about overfished to extinction.

The road we were marching on was very rough in the early days. It was known for its many bordellos to serve the sailors. Now, they are trying to lure businesses back. There are quite a few nice eateries and bars on the strip heading towards the harbor.

The march was maybe a mile and a half long and ended at the Public Dock by the lift bridge. The Knights of Columbus walked to the dock; the bagpipers stayed put at the entrance of the assembly, while the rest walked through.

The proceedings went as follows:

> Posting of the Colors by the Knights of Columbus
> Pledge of Allegiance
> Greeting
> Reading of Scripture
> Prayer Service

The first reading was Genesis 1:19, then Matthew 8:23-27. The prayers were The Lord's Prayer, the Shipmaster's Prayer, the Sailors' Prayer, and Prayer of Blessing of the Boats. These were followed by The Memorial Prayer, the casting of the wreath on the water, Taps, the final blessing, and a closing song by the Mother of Sorrows Men's Choir.

The ceremony was concluded with Bishop Murray and Father Ruggieri boarding a boat and traveling the harbor and river to bless all the boats.

I took a few photos with Bishop Murray, shook hands with Mr. Cordial, thanking him for his hospitality. I waited until the boat with Bishop Murray and Father Ruggieri departed the dock before I left.

I may not agree with everything in the Catholic faith, but they do have very beautiful services. I felt blessed to be invited to their worship.

This annual event of the Blessing of the Fleet Celebration occurs in late May or early June.

# Chapter Three

## A Scene from the Kentucky trip....

We were heading back to Morehead after spending a day in Van Lear touring Butcher Holler the birthplace of Loretta Lynn, a coal mining museum, and driving around Jenny Wiley State Park.

Close to Prestonsburg was road construction that spun me around to another road that I wasn't quite sure where it was heading. Just a short distance later, I spotted a car pulled over on the berm, with the hood open and a lady standing next to it. Being nighttime and out in the country, which is not a good place for anyone to be stranded, I pulled in front of the broken-down car to see what was going on.

I told Lori to roll down her window and ask if the woman needed help. She did, and the lady yelled back, "DO YOU HAVE ANY WATER?" Lori responded with, "WHAT KIND?" I snapped back to Lori, "WHAT KIND? Of course, we got water. What are you talking about, what kind?"

Luckily, I had a jug. I always carry water with me whenever I travel, just a habit of mine, probably picked up from my parents. I got out of the car and was greeted by a dog. As I went to grab the dog, thinking it was the lady's, it ran into the woods.

I approached her and asked if that was her dog. She said, "No, and there is another one in my car that just jumped in. Take a look." HUH? I peered in and, sure enough, there was this cute little dog, all comfy, snuggling in this woman's jacket, with a confident look that said: *You're not kicking me out; I'm going home with you.* It was adorable.

I poured the water into the radiator for her and asked what she was going to do with the dog. She answered, "I guess I am bringing it home to Ma." I slammed her hood shut and asked, "How far you going?" She said, "Only a few miles." I told her we would follow to make sure she didn't break down again. She got in her car and took off like a rocket. We followed in pursuit and, out of nowhere, the other dog reappears in the middle of the freeway, staring at our car, wagging his tail with a look of *Hey, I decided I want to come along with you - PLEASE don't leave me here.* I put on the brakes and my immediate thought was *What the heck...might as well save this dog, also,* but the instant chorus of "NOs" from Nancy, Millard and Lori made me do otherwise, so I just drove around it.

I can imagine those two dogs earlier, walking along the side of the freeway. The big, dumb dog says, *Well what are we going to do? Huh? Huh? What are we going to do?* The little dog says, *Listen, I have a plan:*

*when a car pulls off the road, we're jumping in, but I get the first car. You take the second, understand?* Big dog Replies, *Duh, well, that's dangerous.* Little dog says, *Just shut up and do as I say - got it?*

The first car pulls off the freeway and parks, and the little dog says, *See ya, kid. My opportunity just arrived. You grab the next car out of here.*

As our cars were pulling away, the little dog is saying to himself, *Well, I tried telling that dumb mutt what to do. I'm off the freeway and on to new adventures. Hope he has enough common sense to stay out of the middle of the road.*

The big dumb mutt says to himself, *GEEE, he did it, he did it. He really got in. I shoulda listened and did it, too. OH, OH, here's a car. Hey, car, stop. I want a ride. I don't bite. Please stop!*

# Chapter Four

## Careyisms

Connie, a friend of mine, came up with this term: "Careyism." Definition: Strange and unique things that only happen to Carey that are so unique, they have to be true.

## 680 or 608?

Jeff and I went to Youngstown, Ohio to drop off a carburetor that needed to be rebuilt. After leaving the carb with the mechanic, I asked for directions to Rogers.

Rogers is a small town that has a huge flea market every Friday, with auctions for livestock, food, and household items. I didn't write down the directions because they were fairly simple. The mechanics said to take 680 to Western Reserve to Market. Simple!

Leaving the repair shop, we saw Rt. 680, but I said, "I think the guy said 608." Jeff insisted it was 680. We went back and forth on what route: 608 - 680, 680 - 608. So, I said, "To be sure, let's pull into this beverage drive-through. I will buy us drinks, and ask for directions."

The lady clerk came up to our car and, before placing our order, we asked for directions. She told us to take Rt. 680 - there is no 608. We told her what we wanted and she came back with our drinks.

And the total due was... $6.08...608!

## The Phone Book

The strange and the unexplained always seem to follow me, like in this story about the phone book.

I was heading to Meadville, PA., to visit a friend for the weekend. Meadville is not that far, only about 85 miles from my house. For some reason, I felt that I should bring a Cleveland phone book with me, so I could grab addresses to send post cards, which I am known to do. I thought to myself, *I am only going to Meadville and would be gone just two days. Why am I bringing a phone book to send post cards?* But, I went along with my inner leading and threw it in the car.

I got to Meadville a few hours later. Before going to my friend's, I stopped at a donut shop; it was the first place I saw in town. As I was walking in, I saw a mid-70s Chrysler that was pretty sharp-looking. I saw the owner, an elderly gentleman, about to get in it, and said to him, "Nice-looking car." He told me what year it was and we struck up a conversation. He asked where I was from. I said, "The Cleveland area."

The gentleman replied, "The Cleveland area, huh? By chance, would you happen to have a phone book? I have been wanting one from Cleveland for some time, so I could look up some businesses."

The first place I stopped and this guy asks for a phone book?

I said, "Believe it or not, I do. I brought one along with me and you can have it." He was more than thankful, shook my hand, got in his car, and left.

# Chapter Five

## Beaver Creek,
## Buttermilk Falls and Fish

Dov called and asked, "Hey, do you want to go on a road trip? I need to see trees; I need to get out of the city." He mentioned a few places, like Hocking Hills. I thought about Leesville, Ohio or maybe Tionesta, PA, but all those were too far for the amount of time we had. Instead, we stayed a little closer to home and went to Beaver Creek State Park in Ohio.

Beaver Creek State Park is nine miles south of Rogers, Ohio on Rt.7. Rogers still hosts one of the best flea markets. It's held every Friday, has a small diner inside the grounds, an auction, and the market, which has everything under the sun, from fruits and vegetables to usual and unusual flea market finds. I only stopped briefly at the flea market on the way to Beaver Creek, just enough time to grab a bag of oranges.

Instead of writing about Beaver Creek State Park, read what is written about it from the ODNR website:

*Beaver Creek State Park, in the foothills of the Appalachian Mountains, is one of Ohio's most scenic parks • The park includes Little Beaver Creek, a state and national wild and scenic river, and 2,722 acres of forest wilderness • The rich history of the area invites visitors to explore Gaston's Mill, pioneer village and abandoned canal lock.* (Period was missing)

The thing that hit us the most when we pulled into the park was the smell. It is a pine forest and the smell of pine is so strong, simply wonderful. Just don't park close to the outhouse like we did because the second smell to hit you will be that. It's very peaceful with very few visitors, at least when we were there.

The water in Beaver Creek is clear and perfect for walking through or sitting and cooling. At the time we went, it was extremely low because of a severe drought.

The houses in the pioneer village were locked up, but we were still able to look in the windows to see what life was like back in the early 1800s. The reconstructed village has a school, chapel, house and a few other buildings. They have open house on Saturdays, where they allow you to walk through all of the structures.

We didn't stay too long at the park, as we wanted to continue on with our road trip and take a loop home through Pennsylvania. I'm really not sure what roads we took to get to PA. We zigged and zagged and ended up close to Beaver Falls, PA. and, from there, got on Rt. 18, heading north.

Driving through Beaver Falls, we passed an old train station. Signs were posted "No Trespassing," but I stopped anyway. I didn't venture too far and didn't enter the old abandoned building, but I did snap a few photos, then hurried back to my car.

Right outside of town, just a few miles down the road, is a sign for Buttermilk Falls Nature Area. I asked Dov, "Want to stop and see it?" "Sure, he said." At the first road I saw, I went to turn around and spotted another sign that said FISH FRY – HOMEWOOD VOLUNTEER FIRE DEPARTMENT. July 13th, 5:00 p.m. to 7:30 p.m. I told Dov, "I'm hungry. Let's go to the fish fry and then head back to the falls." We continued on until we saw yet another sign that wasn't well-placed, and this one said FISH FRY this Lent till 7:00 p.m. Dov and I went back and forth. He said, "It's during Lent." I said, "July 13th." I won and continued on.

We guessed at the direction and finally found the Homewood Fire Dept. It also had a big sign that said Fish Fry until 8:00 p.m. Good, I made it in time. But, it was so quiet and hardly anyone around. Maybe it *was* during Lent. I walked into the station and sitting there was a really neat old mid-50s Chevy fire truck. Could they really still be using this relic?

I found the stairs to the basement hall and asked, "Did I miss the fish fry?" Like I actually needed to ask, as the place was empty, and those who remained were busy cleaning. "Yes" was the reply. "We just closed." I said, "Well, I wasn't sure if the fry was for Lent or today, or 7:00 p.m. or at 8:00 p.m." The lady replied, "We used whatever signs we had left." I said, "Well, I could come back in January at 6:00 p.m., if that's OK." She said, "Well, sorry. We don't have any fish, but I will give you for free some macaroni and cheese and coleslaw, if you like." One of the volunteers overheard this and said, "You really want fish. Let me start the fryer back up. It'll take about 15 minutes."

The fish fry dinner included fresh beer-battered haddock, fresh-cut French fries, coleslaw and homemade dessert, with beverage, for $8.00. The fish was excellent.

While waiting, I asked the lady, "Is there a back way to the falls or do I need to get back on the main road?" She said, "Oh, you can park at the abandoned hotel, the Valley Inn." We walked towards the door, so she could point out the direction. I asked if the falls were scenic. She asked, "Have you ever heard of the movie *I am Number Four*?" When she said it, another lady joined in all excited: "They filmed the movie right here at the falls and we watched the whole thing." I asked, "How were you allowed?" "Well, we are the fire department and had to watch the production for safety purposes. My husband met Steven Spielberg and talked with him. It was so exciting to see the falls all lit up and the actors making the movie. And the food....wow! One tent was set up just for all the different coffees and the buffet table was huge with all kinds of food."

My fish was done and they gave us directions once more: "Park at the falling down Valley Inn hotel. You can't miss it. From there, cross the railroad tracks, over the train trestle and you will see a path to the falls." I grabbed my supper and hurried out to explore.

Dov and I parked and, after some guessing, crossed the tracks, found the path and headed to the falls. It was really beautiful, but what is usually a 35-foot flowing fall was just a trickle. It, too, was hard-hit by the drought. I ate my supper right on top of the falls; that's how dry it was. What a really neat experience!

Sunset was fast approaching so, after the fall-top dinner, we hit the road. I got home about 1:00 a.m. from our day trip. I flopped on the couch, turned on cable, flipped through the movie channels, and what did I stumble upon? *I am Number Four*. HEY, I was just there!

# Chapter Six

## Looking for Gators

Walt and I were in Florida back in '99 at a place called Lake Myakka. The flood season was late by a couple of months. It was August and the place looked like a ghost town because of the rising water. The boardwalk and just about the whole park were submerged. This really disappointed us because Walt was hoping to show me an alligator in the wild.

There was only one groundskeeper left, who was just leaving when we arrived. On his way out, he told us there are gators all throughout the park and to be careful, not only because of them, but other animals and reptiles could be floating around. He repeated – BE CAREFUL! This warning was all Walt and I needed to get our curiosity up and our adrenaline flowing. Once the guy left, we were on our merry way, swamp walking and looking for gators. No special gear, just us in our cutoffs. We must have walked around a good hour trudging every which way without one sighting. How disappointing, not one gator, not even a snake!

On our way out of the park, about a half mile or less, were a couple of cars pulled off the road looking over a bridge at something. We thought it was an accident so, of course, we had to get out and investigate. As we approached the crowd, we asked what happened. A guy responded, "Oh nothing. We are just looking at a couple of gators."

Walt and I just started laughing. An hour of walking through a swamp, risking our lives just to see a gator, and there they were, less than a half mile from the park, in plain view.

Find the Sails in Life
Cut the Anchors

# Chapter Seven

## Notes from Boston

Boston - what a city! I'm lovin' it!

It took 10 hours to get here from Cleveland and we stopped twice. Not bad. The part of Massachusetts we drove through is very wooded; it's cold, about 50, and it's August.

The hotel we're staying at is great: Hotel MIT. The elevator looks Star Trek-ish, the furnishings in the room are very retro modern, and the bathtub is huge. After walking around all day and then, our walk back to Cambridge from Boston to save $2 subway fare, oh, about an hour-plus walk – about which the locals lied and said it was 20 minutes - that tub came in handy.

The hotel is right next to a supermarket. What a supermarket. The store has so much variety with aisles and aisles of different ethnic foods.

I really did think Boston would be filled with all white Irish Catholics. Nope! Not at all! Silly me! It is way more international than I expected. Even the lady at the front desk of the hotel, who signed us in, was a foreigner. She was from Columbia. I had such a hard time understanding her. I thought it was weird when she said we could "come play Atari," but I asked where we could play it, anyway. She said "Atari?" Dov interrupted to interpret and said, "NO, she said 'complimentary' not 'Come play Atari.'" OH! Now, THAT made more sense. She was such a friendly lady. She had a headache and asked if I could pray for her, which I did.

Even more surprising is the large Italian section, which I never knew they had, but then it occurred to me that both *Paul Revere* and *Cinderella's* (the latter is the restaurant we had coffee at that served it in mini shot glasses) ended in vowels. Could Paul and Cinderella be Italian? Makes you wonder, huh?

The Italian section had very narrow streets, and all those Italians and those smells, from the delis and restaurants - not the people.

Speaking of smells...at the hotel, they have free computer service. The computers are in a very tiny enclosed room, kind of like a walk-in closet. The lady using the computer next to me smelled like sheep - a herd, not just one. I had to ask her where she was from and she said "Virginia." Hmm, probably the hills of Virginia!

# Here's a Summary of Day Two:

Fun, enjoyment, brief disruption, then back to having fun!

We drove way out to Cape Cod and briefly stopped in Provincetown; I mean *briefly*. Even though I don't live under a rock and I know what is going on, it was still sad to see. This is where the Pilgrims landed, established America, founded it upon biblical principles and religious liberty, and now it's a gathering place for sexual deviants. In America the mighty, the Godly nation, now on display for all tourists and foreigners to see, same-sex couples holding hands, kissing. I won't be back. Boston maybe, as we didn't see any such thing, but Provincetown, NOPE!

Nearby Nauset Beach was great. Clean, white sand; it's really gorgeous, but the parking is $15 before 4:00 p.m. Crazy! So we waited until it was free. After that we went to Plymouth Rock. It's chilling to be standing in the spot where the beginnings of America were being shaped. You could spend a whole day here; we saw what we could in the hour we had.

Here are a few more mental notes I took: Harvard was impressive, Boston was clean and lively with people everywhere, along with bicyclists, and prices were relatively affordable.

Well it's almost 2:30 a.m. and need to sleep. We're waking early and taking the long-cut home because we're stopping in NY City to eat at Katz's Deli. YES - NYC for supper. Dov said they have the best corned beef anywhere. It better be, considering the distance we have to travel.

Signing off from Boston.

## Early Supper in New York City

I didn't take many notes, but this I will tell you: DO NOT attempt to drive through New York City at three in the afternoon. I think it was quicker to get to New York City from Boston than it was to go about 10 feet in New York City traffic.

We ended up getting lost, so I exited in the Bronx to ask directions, which Dov wasn't too happy with, but his protest fell on deaf ears. He was even more unhappy and nervous when the guy I asked for directions to Manhattan said, "Follow me." Dov angrily said, "You don't follow someone you don't know in NY. How do you know where he is taking us?" I said, "Well, he is taking us to where he is going because I am following him." Our guide tuned out to be a true Samaritan. He got us around some nasty traffic jams and only a short distance from Katz's Deli. We never could have done it without him.

Katz's was good. They had real Jews serving the corned beef; they knew what they were doing. Delicious!

It was worth taking the long-cut to eat, but Dov wasn't happy I wanted to take the scenic long-cut home. I mean, it was OK to take a long-cut hours and miles away just for supper to eat corned beef, but not OK to take a scenic long-cut home – nope, not at all. Dov insisted it was to save on the tolls but, even if it was to save on tolls, it would still be scenic. (Yes, "long-cut," the opposite of short-cut, is one of several "Careyisms!" printed in this book – and nowhere else!)

Either way, I won the argument and drove through the Alleghenies, taking the long route home. While Dov snored, the brilliant display of nonstop shooting stars kept me awake and entertained, plus I saved on tolls.

# Chapter Eight

## The Spinning Spatula
## – A Scene from the Manhattan Trip

Traveling as much as I do, it gets costly eating out all the time, plus I miss home-cooked meals. So, no matter where I go, camping, motels or hotels, I always bring my vintage tin picnic basket. It has all the necessary things an Italian survival kit should have: pots, dishes, silverware and, of course, spices, especially Italian seasoning. You would be surprised how creative I can get cooking with this compact setup.

In our hotel room, I went to hang up my coat and noticed an ironing board. It never occurred to me before in my other travels how this would make a perfect table for a hot plate and dishes. Something else was in that closet that struck me. Why didn't I think of that before? I won't tell you what it is until I try it. I don't want you to burn down a hotel and blame me for it.

Knowing how expensive everything is in Manhattan, I really packed for meals this trip. I used one dresser drawer for snacks and set up the ironing board for the hotplate and spices. Dov was really upset at me, though, because the first night, I cooked fish and the whole room smelled. I can only imagine what the housekeepers must have thought.

But, none of the above is what this short story is all about. I wrote all that just to set it up. So, without further ado, here's the spinning spatula story.

## The Spinning Spatula

The Roosevelt Hotel we stayed at was at one time THE hotel. Time has passed it by somewhat, but it is still up there in class. It's elegantly decored with marble, chandeliers, plush seating, a fabulous restaurant and bar.

Dov, who planned this trip, can at times be very reserved around people and certain settings, unlike me; it doesn't matter where I'm at, if I feel a good joke or laugh coming on, I will let it out.

Leaving our room to check out, I asked Dov to help carry things. I grabbed the two duffel bags I had, one in each hand. I gave him the tin picnic basket to carry. He placed it on top of his wheeled suitcase.

We head to the checkout counter, with a line of people before us and behind us. These patrons were very typical of most of the people we encountered in Manhattan: snooty, won't look at you, and definitely don't smile. I'm not sure if they are afraid to ruin their makeup or their face lifts are too tight.

Anyways, it was our turn at the counter; we sign the necessary papers and I head out with Dov in tow with his wheeled suitcase and the tin basket on top. Suddenly, I hear this CRASH that echoed off the marble floors and walls. I turn to find ALL the contents of my survival kit strewn on the floor. Plates, cups, seasonings, and spinning around on the glistening floor was - the spatula.

Everyone smiled and then broke out into a loud laugh. I, for once, was so embarrassed that I ran and hid by one of the information desk clerks. He was a stiff older gentleman, wearing a suit without a wrinkle, who also started laughing and said to me, "That has to be the most perfect sound of crashing dishes I ever heard, just like one of those sound effects in the movies!"

Dov was on his hands and knees in an embarrassed panic, trying to gather everything. I finally decided to help, but not before I said loudly, "How did YOU drop YOUR stuff?" I emphasized "YOU" and "YOUR." He said, "Get over here. I'm not picking this up," and he walked away. I replied, "Fine. I will pick up YOUR stuff!"

We saw many things on that trip, but the two that stick out the most in my mind and will be forever etched in my memory are the sight of the spinning spatula on the marble floor and those people laughing.

It took a dropped tin picnic basket to make them laugh but, boy, did they! Oh, and that spinning spatula....

# Chapter Nine

## The Dark Stranger of Somerville, Texas

Even though I was running extremely low on sleep, my habit of going to bed late kept me wide awake past midnight. While Jimmy slept and Walt unwound watching TV, I went for a long walk. I was on a quest to find a late-night milk shake or float that I had failed to find earlier in the day.

We were staying at the Super 8, which is on the edge of town, one of the last structures before leaving Somerville. The thoroughfare of this mini city is about two and one-half miles long, if that. I just about walked the whole strip. My first stop was Mama's Kitchen. I entered and asked if they had floats. The waitress said "No." I then asked, "Well, do you have Sprite?" "Yes." "Do you have ice cream?" "Yes." "Do you think you can add a couple of lumps of ice cream to my Sprite?" She replied, "Sit down. I will take care of you." A few minutes later, she reappears to tell me they were out of ice cream. Either they were, or my recipe was a bit hard to follow. So, off I went to continue my search.

Next, I walked to a convenience store on the opposite end of town, about the only thing left open. I spied the soda fountain and said to myself, *If I can't find a float, I will build one*. So, I grabbed the 32-ounce cup, filled it with Sprite, and walked around, looking for a small container of ice cream. I found an ice cream cup and asked, "How much?" The clerk said, "They are on sale: two for a dollar." Bought two and plopped them in my Sprite with the help of the worker, who lent me scissors to pry the ice cream out of the cup. He said, "OH, I see what you are doing." I replied, "YES, what a deal: a float for $1.99." I leave.

The temp had cooled down to 88, just an occasional car passing by, no sounds except crickets and a dog barking in the distance; very peaceful. I was enjoying life. I got to the corner of $8^{th}$ and Rt. 36, where the Somerville Museum is located. It was here the dark stranger crossed my path. Actually, it pounced out of the shrubs and immediately attached itself to my leg. I was startled and almost dropped my float. It was a black cat!

I stepped back, not knowing if the thing was rabid. It wouldn't leave me alone, so I scooped out a little ice cream onto the pavement. The cat starting licking it up, and I took off. I got about 15 feet, when the cat caught up with me. It was doing a "figure 8" around my legs, making sure I didn't get away.

Again, I dropped some ice cream. And again, the cat stopped to lick it up, only to hurry and catch up with me again. HMMMM! I tried having a talk with it: "OK, listen. You need to go." That didn't work. Then, I started feeling sorry for the poor critter, who was so skinny. I looked it in the eye and said, "Alright, I have a pork chop back at the motel; follow me." And it did.

We got to the motel and came up with a game plan: we'll go through the back door, but we still have to sneak past the front desk, as we were staying on the first floor. It was just like in the movies. I opened the door. "OK. Ready, let's go." We ran through the hall. At the entrance for the front desk I waved *Hold it*, and I went through first. The lady looked at me, but never looked down as the cat passed. I fumbled with the card to open the door. Nervously, I got it open, shooed the cat in, shut the door. Brilliant! It worked, but how do I explain this to Walt?

So, what did Walt say? Nothing, other than, "OH, a cat!" I grabbed my leftovers I was saving and sat down to feed our guest. It kept pulling the pork chop out of my hand, as I was breaking it up into smaller pieces. The poor little thing was starved. It wasn't that old of a cat, maybe under a year old, maybe a kitten, I don't know. It jumped from bed to bed and made itself at home, very well-mannered. How sad someone had abandoned it; I quickly made that assessment.

In the morning, the rest of the pork chop bone was gnawed to nothing. Didn't know cats chewed bones and didn't know they knew how to get into styrofoam containers, either. And the good news was - no mess was found; we were safe.

When Jimmy woke, he sat straight up and said, "There's a cat!" Walt, teasing him, said, "What cat?" "Right there!" Walt asked me, "Do you see a cat?" "I don't."

We didn't know what to do with it, so I told Jimmy, "Hurry and let it out the back door before the cleaning lady gets here. If the cat is still there when we leave, I will take it."

Fortunately, we parked next to a couple who was just leaving the motel. They were adjusting the boat they were towing. The cat jumped in the boat and was rolling around playing. Walt went up to the couple and explained that it was a stray and said, "If you want it, take it." The cat was nowhere to be seen when we left, so I assumed the couple took it. I was almost hoping the little critter was still around the motel.

In the end, another stranger came and went, and another lasting memory made.

# Chapter Ten

## Nighttime Rainbow

This event took place on Wednesday, July 5th, 2006, 6:30 a.m.

Monday night, into Tuesday morning, there was a rainstorm with a spectacular display of lightning. I went to the CEI break-wall in Eastlake, Ohio to view the light show and rain coming off of Lake Erie. I saw something that I am not sure anyone ever has.

Over the lake was a reddish rainbow. It would eerily come and go. My first thought was that it might be the streetlights reflecting off the lake or rain. But, having been to the break-wall countless times while it rained, I've never witnessed this phenomenon before, so I quickly dismissed that thought. Still not sure what was causing it.

A reddish rainbow over the lake at night!

# Chapter Eleven

## Short Trips

### Amish Country, Ohio

Holmes County, the world's largest Amish community, is just a short drive from Cleveland, Ohio. It seems like you're back in time. In fact, I asked Lori, who went with me on this day trip, if she liked the place, and all she said was "everything is so old." Not sure if that meant she liked it or not, but I know I did.

Another place we visited was Sugarcreek, nicknamed "The Little Switzerland of Ohio." Many of the buildings in the village look like the Old World.

Two things really got my attention: one was the tanning salon. I didn't even know the Amish got undressed! Number two was the unusual location of a campsite in Sugarcreek. With all the land available, you would never expect to find a campsite behind a small strip mall in a gravel lot with no trees. Strange location, indeed!

# Brunswick, Ohio

## Sometimes group outings don't work out, like when we went to Mapleside Farms in Brunswick

This was supposed to be a fun Christmas outing with the gang, but it turned into a Christmas nightmare not to remember. I told the group we were going to Mapleside Farms for dinner, followed by a jaunt to the French Creek District in Avon, Ohio to browse the antique and trinket shops for Christmas gifts.

Mapleside Farms is a rustic-style restaurant with an apple orchard and is always nicely decorated for Christmas. Well, someone in our group thought we were going to eat at a real farm; hence, she wore BIG boots and a HEAVY coat. Someone else - whom I won't mention his name, either - took his sleeping pills at 7:00 p.m. and battled the rest of the night to stay awake. I asked him, "Why would you take sleeping pills at 7:00 p.m.?" He replied, "I thought I might forget to take them later." Then there was Princess Charming, yelling at me through the whole outing because she wanted to get home early. And, on top of all that, heading to Avon from Mapleside, I got us lost in the middle of nowhere, with nothing around but farms and a few scattered houses.

I pulled into someone's drive at dark and knocked on their door for directions, which everyone thought I was nuts for doing. The house I picked....what did it have on the garage door? The family name: The house of the DULLS – yes, the Dulls. How appropriate.

Oh, by the time we got to Avon, all the stores had closed. At least the dinner was good.

Never Surrender
Your Quiet Place

# Chapter Twelve

## The Car Trip

An elderly lady I know, who annually goes to Florida for the winter months, called and asked if I could drive her car back home to Ohio. She would fly me to Florida, pay all expenses and give me two days to return her car while she takes a flight home. This is my recount of that trip.

There we were, in Cleveland Hopkins Airport, waiting our turn to go through "Checkpoint Charlie," when I asked a lady security guard if I could take a picture of the display case of confiscated weapons security had taken from passengers about to board. *Sure*, she nodded. Well, guess she didn't know the rules. As the flash from my camera went off, so did another security guard, who barked at me, "WHY DID YOU TAKE THAT PICTURE?" So, I pointed out the lady who had said it was okay. Regardless of what I said or who said what, as we approached our turn to be scanned, we were pulled from the line: "YOU two over here!"

I guess it didn't help matters that Dov does look like he's of Middle Eastern descent, coupled with his backpack and my dark hair and complexion and, of course, camera; not sure what that has to do with anything, but it mattered to them. They separated us and, then, the inter-rogation began.

"SO, who are you? Where are you going? How long have you known him?" Blah, blah, blah. "I'm heading to Florida to drive a car back to Ohio for an elderly lady I know." They tried their best to make me slip up. "So, you're buying the car." "Why did she give you the car?" "You're driving the car back for her" and about another twenty variations of the same question. Then, the inter-rogator took out some cloth and started wiping my camera and shoes.

"How long have you worked with fertilizer?" That question killed me and the answer I gave was even worse; sometimes, I don't know what my brain is going to throw out. I said, "I work with insecticides and pesticides," which I don't but, like I said, I never know what's going to come out of me. My reply even stumped the guy and put a dumb look on his face. Then, the interrogator excused himself and met his partner halfway between Dov and me; they did some talking and switched.

Now I had Dov's interrogator. Just about the same questions. But, this time, I plugged my website. The one guy asked me, "So, why is your friend so nervous and anxious?" I said, "Maybe he used to do a lot of drugs...I don't know." I told Dov this, and he said, "Thanks a lot for selling me out like that." I replied, "I didn't know what else to say." He snapped back, "You could have told him I have anxiety." "Yeah, I guess I could have. Just didn't think of it." They finally were convinced we were not terrorists, but tourists, handed our stuff back, and we were free to roam about the country.

In a way, I was glad they took up so much of our time because our plane was an hour late. Hey, my thinking is *Much better being put through a quiz and exam to pass time than sitting, waiting for a late-arriving plane.*

We still had some time to kill, so we walked around Hopkins. And, sure enough, following behind were... "thee interrogators." They continued to keep an eye on us. The world was made so much safer because of their actions.

It was finally time to board and, as we were about to enter the plane, it was photo-op time. I got very lucky. Walking right behind us was a Japanese couple. As you know, Japanese people always carry cameras and know how to use them. I handed the man my camera and he took an excellent photo of us entering the plane. It's always *Cross your fingers and hope the photo turns out* whenever you ask someone, but this one was well-taken. Dov and I looked like real terrorists, umm, I mean tourists.

We took our seats and I made this observation: have you ever noticed how eerily quiet airports and plane rides are? I remarked to Dov, "Look at these people, how sullen they are. You'd think they would be laughing and living it up. This could be their last flight. Hey, you never know."

We sat next to a guy that flies thousands of miles a year. I asked Dov to ask him if he had TB; he didn't, which was a good thing.

The other observation I made was about the snack they served us. I had to take a photo of it. The snack was so small, I used a telephoto lens to snap the picture. *Continental*'s new motto should be "Work hard - Fly right - Eat little." I mean, the coffee was a little bigger than a Dixie cup, and the mini pretzels were so small, tweezers were needed to pick them up. Cost cutting, or are they trying to make the planes lighter?

Our flight was smooth and uneventful all the way to Florida.

Jumping ahead, what do I think of Florida?

**One**: The first thing that strikes me is AIR CONDITIONING. I hate air conditioning; everywhere and everything has air conditioning, even golf carts. Those people down there run from their air conditioned houses, hurry up to their air conditioned cars, off to their air conditioned stores or places of work, then back home to their air conditioned houses. That's all they do, is run to air conditioners. They are prisoners. Why would you live in such a place?

I never use air conditioning, not even in the car. Dov was complaining as we were driving: "Let's turn on the air." I said, "It's not too bad. It's only 99 degrees out," and it was early June.

**Two**: The friend we met in Florida pointed this out: she said, "Did you notice how people down here wear long pants and sweaters?" She was right. Her sister, who came with her to the airport to pick us up, wore a sweater and long pants, probably from being cold from the air conditioning. And, this lady where we were staying at came out of her frosty apartment to have a smoke and chat with us. What did she have draped around her? A blanket! OK, maybe wearing it in her igloo, but outside with it being a blast furnace - I didn't understand that.

**Three**: Heat stroke/cold shock. My body never adjusted to the Arctic cold inside to the hellish hot outside. It made me dizzy.

**Four**: The air is so humid and thick that, even late at night, it feels like you could grab it.

**Five**: Traffic, traffic, and more traffic. No matter where you go in Florida, you face traffic.

**Six**: Corporations have invaded. It was hard to find locally-owned and operated stores and restaurants down there; it's mostly corporations.

**Seven**: Is anybody actually born in Florida? Everyone seems to be transplants.

After the formalities at the airport, the food fiasco started. Our lady friend asked if we were hungry. *Of course* we were, but I was not prepared for what transpired the next five hours. "Okay, I will take you out to eat first, then take you to where we are staying. No, let's go to where we are staying, and then eat. No, let's unpack first, then eat. No, let's eat where we are staying. No, let's eat on the way home." In between all that, she asked what I was hungry for. Well, we were in Florida and all that water made me think seafood; besides, the only other Florida food I know is oranges and I wasn't in the mood for that.

To make a long story short, we ate five hours later, close to 10:00 p.m., and not much was left open, other than a restaurant miles from where we were staying. It got even screwier: the lady friend blamed me for wanting fish because we had to drive so far and also, because she didn't like her clam chowder. She insisted they put cayenne pepper in it. The waiter was tired of arguing with her because they don't use pepper in chowder; he finally took it off the bill.

We stayed the night, packed her car, and started our journey back to Ohio in the morning, by first stopping at Clearwater's gorgeous white sand beaches. And, if you never have seen white sand, well, let me tell you: it's white! Even though the sky was overcast and cloudy, the sand was still blinding. I needed sunglasses. Then there is a sign for Pier 60 that costs 50, 50 cents that is. They let you walk halfway on the pier; then, in the middle, is a gate where they charge. They also have sun umbrellas you can rent; if I heard correctly, they cost $25 to sit under. Only in the land of the free does everything cost something.

After Clearwater, we journeyed across Florida: Rt. 41 to 75 to 301, up to 95, and headed into Georgia. Kind of getting ahead again, but I was very impressed with the scenery along Georgia's coast. I always thought Georgia was mostly farmlands and boring. It is beautiful! Another place I have to revisit.

OK, back to chronological order. Even though I said I don't like air conditioning, I do hate being hot and sticky. I just needed to cool off and get cleaned. So, we headed to the coast of Georgia towards the islands - I believe St. Simons Island - to find a beach where I could jump in and wash up.

We located a beach, but there were "No Swimming" signs posted because the conditions weren't right. So, we ventured further to the next beach. It was just about dark when we arrived. Walking towards the beach, I spotted the rinse-off showers outside the restrooms and thought it was safer to use than swimming at night. I soaped up, using shampoo, and took a chilly outside shower. I don't think these are really intended for this purpose and I don't necessarily endorse a lot of what I do, so don't go trying this stuff and say "Carey does it," 'cause you're on your own. Somehow, though, I always find a way to stay clean. If it's not a rinse-off shower, it's a birdbath or someone's backyard hose.

I have to add this funny tidbit: As we were walking towards the ocean, I was in one of my silly moods. I told Dov, "Watch this." I approached this guy and asked him in a very serious, confused look, "Is this Lake Erie?" He was a foreigner and started laughing at me and said, "OH, NO - this is bigga water," and walked away from me, still chuckling.

After my shower, we hit the highway to start making up lost time. But, I missed a turn and ended up in a dead end: to be exact, a gated community. There was a car in front of us, showing his pass, so security would lift the gate. I decided to tailgate the car, right past the guard, into this exclusive resort-like place. I told Dov we'd keep going 'til they stop us, which they never did. So, we took a drive through the grounds. WOW, what a place! I just wish we'd had more time, so I could have walked around and taken more pictures. Opportunities like this don't come often.

We finally found our way out of the amazing maze and back to the common people. About a half-mile away, I stopped at a convenience mart for directions and asked, "Exactly what was that place we were at?" The guy said that that is where the top three percent live. He mentioned some Georgia and nationally-known bigwigs.

Their names escape me but, I'm telling you, the vision of those houses won't.

We left Tampa at 1:30 p.m. and, still traveling on Rt. 95, got to mid-Georgia by 9:00 p.m. Not bad. When Dov saw the sign "Savannah," he remarked, "I heard that that city has really old southern-style houses." I said, "I heard the same thing." You know what comes next. We exited the freeway and headed to Savannah. And, what we heard was correct.

I was surprised that, on a Wednesday night, the little city was really hopping. Just about every bar had a band playing. This one street was blocked and music was blaring from it, people walking around; it was very lively. The layout was different than other cities that usually have only one square. On this one street, there were about five squares in a row. There was a theater with the name "SCAD" in lights and we even saw a security car with the name "Scad" on it. What's a Scad?

Being somewhat short of cash and not dressed properly, we decided not to eat at the nightclubs or bars and, BOY, was that a mistake. A hard lesson was learned here. We asked someone where to eat and they directed us to the edge of town, where all the corporate restaurants gathered. No, thank you! We headed out hungry, but thinking *Next exit, we can eat*. Yeah, right!

This is a really sad commentary on what has happened to the independent truck stops and restaurants. America had better get a handle on this and avoid the corporate restaurants before there is no choice but these artery-clogging conveyor belts. Now, back to the story!

So, there we were in the land of Dixie, amongst the corporate row, trying to find something that said *real* food, not *fast*. No luck. For the next six and one-half hours and three states, we traveled, looking for an elusive meal. Sure, we found 297 Waffle Houses and places of that nature, but we were looking for real food.

Every exit, we would get off to look for a place to eat, with no luck, so, back on and head to the next one. This went on for mile after mile and added so much time to the trip. Not one truck stop, not one mom and pop diner, nothing but fast food! I don't get it. What happened to truck stops? Don't truckers still eat?

It was about 5:00 a.m. when I exited once again, in a town called Hendersonville, NC. About to succumb from hunger, I apologized to Dov and said, "I can't do it any longer. There's a Denny's, but first, let's take a quick peek through town, just in case. The whole town was asleep, no one stirring. Somehow, I got lost and couldn't find the way back. I think it was God's intervention that stopped me from eating there because, suddenly, out of nowhere, a minivan appeared. I waved him down and asked, "How do we get back to Denny's? We're lost." He said, "Ya hungry?" *Starving*, more like it. "Well now, if

I were you, I'd head to the Mustang Café, which will be open in a few minutes. Follow me." This was almost like a scene from the fabled movie Bullitt. This minivan took off so fast, I had a hard time following him. He got us a street away from the Mustang, pointed, and took off. Do angels drive minivans?

Well, I am surprised the locals didn't call the law on me to check for drugs. I walked in and had a laughing spell that came out of nowhere, a real laugh time. Lack of sleep made me loopy and they looked so redneck-ish. Dov was horrified they would shoot us. I just couldn't help it. Finally, I stopped laughing long enough to order.

So what did I think of the Mustang Café? These are the mental notes I took:

The place was quaint, where locals gather for a sunrise breakfast. The cook was not your typical-looking cook: tight jeans, nice blouse, makeup - she looked like she was ready for a night out. She turned out to be a very good cook. The omelet and hash browns were wonderful. Thumbs up!

I could write about the "ghetto-tel" we stayed at after the Mustang breakfast, but will only quickly say the place was a dump. Another lesson I have learned traveling is, if you see in the lobby of a hotel or motel statues of humans with elephant heads, three-headed gods, and incense burning, it's not the place to stay. And, I can almost guarantee Americans don't own it.

In conclusion, we traveled nine states in two days, from Cleveland Hopkins airport to the airport and City of Tampa, to the white sandy beaches of Clearwater, Florida, to the Georgia coast, where islands and marshes exist, to a gated community where the top three percent live, to the southern historic charm of Savannah and the inner-city poor section, to the freeways and highways of South and North Carolina, to the breathtaking mountains of North Carolina, Tennessee, and Virginia, to the Country Music Highway Rt. 23 of Kentucky, to the power plants and oil refineries along the Ohio River in West Virginia and Ohio, to the light and blight of Huntington, West Virginia, to the twisty two-lane roads of Southern Ohio through Wayne National Forest, to the little City of Jackson, Ohio, to Rt. 23 through Circleville, home of the Pumpkin show, and Columbus, the capital of Ohio and, finally, onward to home we traveled.

What a road trip it was. How did we accomplish all that and manage to visit two friends, one in Morehead, Kentucky and another in Jackson, Ohio? Simple: sleep little, drink coffee, and drive fast. I don't necessarily endorse this recipe for everybody, but it works for me.

**Side Note**: In the email I received about my flight to Florida was a 1-800 number that said *Please call to reconfirm your flight.* I called it, followed the menu: Press one for this, two for that...you know how that goes. Finally, I pressed the number to reconfirm the flight and what did the recording say? "You do not need to reconfirm your ticket." After five minutes of prompts!

# Chapter Thirteen

## The Toilet Incident

Chuck, Walt and I were staying at Babington's campground in Hillsboro, Ohio. It was morning, so we headed to the restroom before venturing out for the day. I was the last one to enter. Walt was already at the sink, shaving. I joined him at the other sink.

I found a Sweetheart soap wrapper on the sink I was using and tossed it over the toilet stall that Chuck was in, and said, "Here, this is for you, Sweetheart." He said in a comical voice, "That's OK," and tossed it back. I, in turn, threw it right back over. Again, it came back with another "Hey, that's OK. You keep it."

I then saw a pair of swim trunks sitting on a bench, tossed them over the toilet stall and said, "Well, what about these? Are these yours?" They came flying back with "HEY, these aren't mine." I was now rolling, and Walt, well, he kept shaving between his laughs.

I found a few more things and tossed them over. As fast as I would toss them, they would come right back with constant "HEYs." I went outside and found a long branch with leaves and shook it over the stall, and said, "What about this? Is this yours?"

51

Then, I took the bench and slid it under the stall repeatedly. I was in hysterics now, as I saw Chuck's feet jump up and down while he was sitting, with "STOP, STOP it already." I had enough fun torturing Chuck and went to finish washing up.

Just then, Chuck enters the restroom and says, "What's taking you guys so long?" I just about died. It wasn't Chuck in the toilet stall. About the same time, the toilet door swings violently open. A man rushes out, gets right in my face, and angrily shouts, "IF YOU HAD TO GO THAT BAD, WHY DIDN'T YOU TELL ME?" Then he stormed out.

I was beyond embarrassed and nervous, and sheepishly asked, "Walt, why didn't you tell me?" "Oh, I thought you knew it wasn't Chuck. I thought it was hilarious."

I hurried up to our vehicle and sank low into my seat until we pulled out, thinking for sure the guy was going to hunt me down.

# Chapter Fourteen

## I Love a Parade

Dad, Bruce and I were returning from a trip visiting Emerson Babington, who owns a campground in Hillsboro, Ohio. I've been to Hillsboro and Rocky Fork Lake numerous times. Instead of traveling the same route home, I decided to try a different way. It was a little longer in mileage, and somewhat slower, but refreshing to see new things.

Before getting to Columbus, my new route had us driving through the town of Obetz. I came upon stopped traffic with people sitting alongside the road. I asked someone, "What's going on?" The man replied, "It's the Zucchini Festival Parade." I then asked Dad and Bruce if they wanted to park and watch it, or should we just keep going? Both wanted to get home, and I gladly agreed with them.

I put the Go-Go Bus in reverse, backed up a bit, drove through a parking lot, down an alley, a small side street and up ahead...clear sailing, we're saved - a main road out of here. I zoomed onto it, then noticed how quiet the road was. There was no traffic; not one vehicle. It was even odder that everyone was out on their porch or sitting on lawn chairs, waving at us. I get waves and thumbs-up all the time, driving the Go-Go Bus, but this was a little different.

It finally dawned on us: HEY, WE'RE ON THE PARADE ROUTE! The people waving at us probably thought we were the start of the parade. Dad just started laughing and waving back. I panicked and took the first exit I saw. And, where did it bring us? Right back to the barricade I first came upon. I threw up my arms in surrender, shut off the Bus, sat back and enjoyed the parade.

The road is a good companion
But has never cured a lonely heart

# Chapter Fifteen

## Easter 2010

Easter 2010 was quite unorthodox – umm, not in a religious way - I mean in the way I usually celebrate it.

Dov and I wanted to take a short trip to anywhere, just to get out and about, and I also wanted to attend Easter service. My thinking was *If I take an overnight road trip and sleep in the Go-Go Bus, I will wake up in time and attend any church I see; but, if I stay home, I will sleep in and wake up according to my normal schedule and miss church.* Makes sense, right?

Dov suggested Oberlin. Why Oberlin? It's a lively lil' college town with coffee shops, secondhand stores, even a five-and-dime. I looked at the map and saw that it was near Findley State Park. Perfect. We would hang out, then camp out.

We get to Oberlin, but it was very quiet. No one was around - coffee shops empty, some even closed. That's when we had the revelation: it's Easter and spring break, this is a college town, and everyone went home for the holiday. So, we took a 10-minute driving tour of Oberlin, looking at the beautiful old houses and buildings on campus, which are just as old and ornate, then headed to Findley State Park to camp.

The admission at Findley was $23 for a campsite, which surprised us, to see a fee during the off season. Like in Oberlin, no one was around, so you paid using the honor system, depositing money through a slot on the door at the camp office. Both of us thought it was crazy to pay just for an overnight parking space but, even if I wanted to, all I had was a credit card. We weren't sure what to do; eventually, our decision was to enter without paying.

After doing 12 loops around the campground, I found a site I liked. It was actually the very first spot we passed. I unloaded a few things, then went looking for firewood, while Dov stayed behind and smoked. After returning from the firewood expedition, Dov tells me, "I'm embarrassed...we can't stay. I have a bad stomach-ache. It was probably from eating too much cheese." All this driving around, looking for a site, setting up, and he wanted to leave? I told him I would make something to eat that would calm his stomach. So, I threw a couple of pork bones on the fire. It fixed him right up.

When our fire died down, I thought I could drag over this fairly large log that was right by our site and toss it in. When the log was moved, a flock of birds nesting above were disturbed, but these were no ordinary birds: they were GIGANTIC! The noise they made with their wings was frightening. Dov freaked and got in the Go-Go Bus. He even locked the doors. Then, I panicked and joined him. It wasn't from being worried that they may swoop down and eat me, but that they may unload on my head. They had to be buzzards, or maybe pterodactyls.

We finished dinner, then went for a night hike and checked out the lake. When we returned, Dov and I debated whether we should stay or leave. Dov said, "It is the Lord's Day and I don't think we should stay without paying. Would you get mad if I told you to leave?" I gave him my political spiel why staying wasn't stealing, but we left, anyways.

We drove back towards the town of Wellington to find a place for the night. At the main intersection, I saw a cop. He was pulling into the city hall/police station. I stopped right next to him and asked, "Is there any roadside rest or a place I could park to sleep?" The patrolman answered, "Sure, right here." Then, I asked, "How long can I sleep for?" He said, "I don't care how long you stay. Just park over there - it may be quieter."

So, I pulled into this huge, adjacent lot. Finding a place to park was easy, but too bad getting sound sleep wasn't. I thought it was supposed to be quieter here... I pulled all the shades. Dov slept up front and I went to the back, crawled under my sleeping bag, and dozed off. Dov wakes me up and says, "Carey, I can't sleep with all these gas fumes." I was so out of it; I remember telling him, "Just open the kitchen window."

I fall back to sleep, and it started: every 20 minutes, another train rumbled through, blowing its horn. This continued the entire morning. I fall back to sleep again.

At 5:00 a.m. my phone rings. At 5:15 a.m. it rings again. It's Mom. She called twice, so I had to answer. "Carey, did you eat? I have chicken wings." Then, at about 8:00 a.m. 'til about 8:30 a.m., siren after siren after siren. I thought I was in East Cleveland. Fall back to sleep. At 8:45 a.m., someone parks next to me. I peek out in time to see some woman getting out of her car. I am thinking, *This HUGE lot, I mean HUGE lot, no one here, not one car, and she has to park on top of me!* Just weird.

I give up and get up at 9:00 a.m.; besides, it's Easter morning and time to find a church. It was absolutely beyond beautiful weather. Dov and I took a walk to find a bathroom and coffee. Thank goodness there was a small diner open. We walk back to the Bus and notice the huge parking lot we slept in was the back of a church. How about that!

Instantly, Dov said, "I think we did the right thing by leaving the park." This definitely had to be a sign from God. We didn't have to find a church - we are already at one. You can't plan things like this.

The church was a United Methodist. It was beautiful inside, but not overly-done, with an older feel to it. They still use an organ with a choir. It was a very nice worship service. Before they started, the pastor, Pastor Lea Mahan, came over to greet us. I told her I slept in the parking lot in the purple bus. She said, "I know. I parked next to you." I said, "That was you? I was wondering why someone parked so close to me." She responded with, "I did it on purpose." Hmm!!!!

One more interesting tidbit...We sat in the last pew in the back. Next to me was a gentleman with such a warm and friendly spirit. Throughout the service, he was explaining to me how they do things, what to expect and who everyone was. His name was Marvin. They had a short break, like a lot of churches do, where you greet and shake hands with someone. The guy in front of me turns around and introduces himself as Marvin. I turn to my right and ask the guy sitting next to me, "What's your name again?" "Marvin." "Marvin. And, what's that man's name, sitting in front of me?" "Marvin." I said, "I never met a Marvin in my life and I am sitting by two!" He replied, "Well, you know another Marvin?" "I do!" "Sure: Marvin Gardens in Monopoly!"

Just a fabulous little getaway, and something I didn't plan. I guess you could say God-ordained.

# Chapter Sixteen

## New York City Traffic

I remember the first time I went to NY City, back in the late 80s. A few friends and I decided to take an unplanned midnight road trip there on a cold Saturday in January. We arrived in early morning. I had fallen asleep and awoke to fogged windows and U2 singing on the radio: "I still haven't found what I'm looking for." As I cleared the windows to look out, I was just awed by the size of these enormous skyscrapers and felt so insignificant. Much has changed since then, most noticeably the absence of the Twin Towers, and all the events surrounding 911.

This recent trip to NY, Dov and I arrived about 8:00 p.m. on a Friday night. Though I was just in NY the previous August, I felt anxiety, ever so briefly, but YES, I felt it. That August visit was much different, as we were in Boston and decided to swing by the Big Apple just for the afternoon. I didn't have much time to think of where I was going because it was totally unplanned, but this trip I knew I would be staying for three days in midtown Manhattan.

As we approached NY from NJ, the traffic became more congested, then slowed to a crawl, then just stopped and, every so often, it would inch up. It was here that I felt that apprehension of *What if there was an attack or an emergency? No way would anyone be able to leave this mess.*

Instead of fighting traffic or attempting to maneuver through the tangle, as some tried, I just kicked back and waited for my turn to move up. We exited the Lincoln Tunnel and weren't sure if we were heading in the right direction. But, it didn't matter - we had to go with the flow of traffic. It's impossible to pull over, and very difficult to ask for directions, either from people not speaking English, not living in the city, or just plain rudeness.

Cars, buses, trucks, cabs, motorcycles, people walking, riding bikes, more cars, more buses, more trucks, more cabs, more motorcycles, more people walking, riding bikes, people, people, people, cars, cars, cars all over the place! Unless you've experienced NY on a Friday night, you just won't understand.

We found out we were going the wrong way to the hotel, according to the map we brought along. So, I did a U-turn on a divided, secondary road that was not as busy. But, driving to the hotel, every street, street corner, and sidewalk was crowded. People lined the sidewalks, either walking or dining outside of restaurants and coffee shops and, of course, the cars, buses and cabs everywhere.

Before arriving at our destination at the Roosevelt Hotel, we needed to find a place to park the car. Having no luck finding a place under $200 for our three-day stay that was close by, we opted to have it parked at the hotel.

As we pulled up and stopped, I marveled how the valet handled the madness. The traffic was unbearable, cars pulling in and out of the hotel, parking cars, opening doors, handing out parking passes. Throughout this craziness, they kept their cool and went about their business, as if it was a lazy day in small-town America. To me, it was just plain nuts!

We loaded our gear on the cart they wheeled out for us but, to avoid the tip, we took our baggage in ourselves. I'm sure they were not used to this, as everyone staying at the Roosevelt must have had money, and lots of it. Once entering the marbled lobby, the pace slowed and, viewing the swank décor, I felt much more at ease. The laid-back atmosphere was far different from the madness outside those doors. It was like the stillness inside the eye of a hurricane!

# Chapter Seventeen

## Clifton Gorge, Clifton Mill and Yellow Springs, Ohio - Review 2013

The first time I visited Clifton was in '97. What I remember about the place is exactly the same, and the same as it was probably 100 or more years ago. Not kidding, either. It has quite a few historical buildings, including a blacksmith shop and an opera house that still holds events. Population of this tiny village is about 150.

This past visit I went to Clifton Mill for breakfast as I usually do when in the area. Clifton Mill is one of the largest water-powered grist mills still in existence. The restaurant has rustic charm, with all kinds of old knick-knacks and antiques hanging from the ceiling and on display throughout. It also has a nice little gift shop. The view from the dining area overlooks the Little Miami River - and it's spectacular!

The pancakes which I always order here are still served so large that I could only finish one in the stack of two. I ordered mine with chocolate chips. Wow, so good, but who could eat two?

During Christmas, they light the mill with 32 million lights. Who counted them all? Don't know, but that's what they say.

Next door is their 1940s Gas Station Museum, filled with original products from that era.

After breakfast, it was off to nearby Clifton Gorge, named at one time by *National Geographic* as one of the most beautiful places in America. The trail is fairly easy to hike and the beauty makes it even easier.

On the edge of the trail, I noticed a small piece of glass from a bottle. I had to investigate. So, I got off the trail that is clearly marked "Danger: Steep Cliffs - Stay on Path." I found an area that is strewn with bits and pieces of OLD pottery and bottles. The way the glass was made, the pieces had to date back to mid- to late 1800s. I searched, but came up with nothing whole.

I ended my hike, then went to the town of Yellow Springs. The Go-Go Bus fit right in and even got a new nickname. Someone called it "The New Age Mystery Machine." Yellow Springs looks like a hippie retirement center, but enjoyable for all. Head shops, tie dye, mixed in with other fun trinket shops, art galleries and clothing stores. There is a variety of cafés, a few restaurants and food vendors on the street, with usual and unusual fare, such as goat curry.

All three places are worth visiting.

# Chapter Eighteen

## The Costly Resort

Ray and I were on vacation in Orlando, Florida. We had minimal funds for this trip. The majority of our money was spent on the resort, gas, and food, with little else to spare.

The resort was beautiful, but it had one major drawback. There was a charge for everything. Needed more towels? There was an extra charge. Sheets changed? Extra charge! More soap? Extra charge! Everything, I mean everything, was extra.

A few days into our week-long stay, our clothes needed cleaning. I came up with the brilliant idea to use the whirlpool tub in our suite as our washing machine, to save money. Ray thought I was nuts, but he relinquished. I went through with the plan, using shampoo as our laundry detergent.

It was hard work, bending over the steaming tub, swirling the clothes around, pulling out an occasional sock that got sucked in, and wasted a lot of time. I got them as clean as I could. Then, we drained the tub and it was time to rinse them. Same scenario: swirl the clothes around, pulling out those that got sucked in, while profusely sweating.

The clothes looked OK, but the tub – well, it had a ring around it that we never did completely remove, and the pump – well, it was a little noisier. Whoops.

After washing, Ray said, "You do realize that we still have to spend some money because these clothes will never dry; it's way too humid." So, we grabbed the wet clothes and headed to the laundry room of the resort. We go to use the dryers and I just about passed out from laughing so hard, and Ray, well… he wanted to choke me.

The washers and dryers were free!

# Chapter Nineteen

## My Review of the Pemberville Free Fair

Pemberville is a small town. It has one gas station, a short main street, a couple of churches, and neatly-maintained older houses. It is about 100 miles west of Cleveland. I read about this fair in an Ohio festivals brochure. The 65-year-old fair is billed as one of the last free fairs in Ohio. I was curious if it was included in the brochure because it's a decent fair or because it was free, or both.

I found out the Pemberville Free Fair is not your typical fair. It is small and has little in the way of the usual fair offerings, which is surprising, being in the middle of farm country. But, it was free! Did I mention that already? It is a nice family event, one that I recommend.

I went on the last day, so a lot of the booths had packed up, including most of the animals. But, I did get to see one sheep, three hens, three rabbits and the quilt display in the school gymnasium. I enjoyed looking at the old parquet floor and how it was flawlessly urethaned. I also enjoyed looking at the quilts.

After the quilt display, I went to a small building, where the baked goodies and produce were judged. The zucchinis got my attention. They were huge! I was lucky to be standing there at that precise time because a lady who was gathering her vegetables grabbed a large zucchini she had entered. The way it was being held, I just had to ask, "How heavy?" She let me hold it and I estimated it to be about seven pounds. OK, I lied. The minute I got home, I weighed it – whoops, I'm getting ahead. We talked briefly about what she does with her zucchinis. She makes zucchini bread, pies, casseroles and other dishes.

From the produce and baked goods display, I went into another building that had photos, miscellaneous crafts and floral displays. And, guess who I bumped into? Why, the lady with the zucchini. She saw her friends and asked if they wanted her zucchini. When they said "No," she offered it to me. She must have seen my eyes light up. I said of course I would take it. Then, she asked how about cucumbers? Sure. Tomatoes? Yes! What about two pumpkins? Absolutely!

I hurried to the car to drop off the vegetables, so I could meet her back at the produce display to grab the pumpkins. Her name was Sandy. She didn't want anything in return, but I still gave her a Go-Go Handy Pack Bag.

Sandy, if you're out there: Thanks, again!

In summary: free fair, free zucchini, free cucumbers, free pumpkins, free tomatoes...OH, and free parking. Life is good!

Secure Your Dreams
Flee From Negative People

# Chapter Twenty

## The Cleveland Submarine

Aqua Amigos is a diving club. They have made me an honorary member, or maybe more like, they allow me to attend their club functions, even if I can only barely swim, let alone dive, though I have been to plenty of dives to eat.

One of their meetings was held in Cleveland at the site of the *USS Cod*, the WWII-era submarine. It was held after public tours ended, so we were able to spend as much time on the sub as we liked, with no supervision.

For those who have never been on a sub, especially an old one, you need to, to truly appreciate what those men had to put up with. Creature comforts were just about non-existent, and space - very cramped. It held a crew of 97 men. Hot bunking and sharing bunks was common. Canned food was stored everywhere, even by the engines. Just incredible, the amount of stuff crammed in this vessel.

The *USS Cod* was the first of the new big subs at 312 feet in length. It held 116,000 gallons of fuel, with a top surface speed of 24 mph, and a top submerged speed of 10 mph. It was a very successful sub, having lost only one submariner, who was washed overboard. She sank about a dozen enemy warships and merchant ships, and damaged many others during WWII.

If ever in the Cleveland area, I recommend taking this tour.

# Chapter Twenty One

## Elk Viewing

When I travel, seldom do I follow a straight line, and rarely do I travel the same course twice. I try to cram in as much as possible on any trip I take. Such was the case driving back from New York City. On the way there, we stopped at a rest area in PA. I spotted brochures for elk viewing, so, of course, I made a mental note to investigate that on the way home.

Entering Pennsylvania on the return trip, we exited and went to a PA welcome center. I told the attendant we wanted to see elk. So, she mapped out a route and gave us brochures for the Pennsylvania Wilds and Elk Scenic Drive. She even gave me a brochure on quilts. Not sure what that has to do with elk viewing, unless I am starting to look old, and she thought maybe I need one for my rocker.

The course written out was as such: get back on Rt. 80, exit on 180 N to Williamsport, Rt. 220 W, 120 W, 949 S, and that would lead us back to Rt. 80. We followed those directions exactly. What a stark contrast from the noisy, people-filled, skyscraper city to the quiet solitude of the lush green mountains – just beautiful!

We drive past Williamsport a ways and there it was: an ELK sign. I was excited. OK, maybe no big deal but, to me, it was a sign, a sign we were on the right course, and a sign that there are elk.

The sign was planted at a small roadside rest next to a river. I walked to the riverbank, but Dov didn't follow. He was concerned by another sign, this one warning in red letters DANGER! HORNETS NESTING IN GROUND! Heck, I just tiptoed gingerly and ignored it. I enjoyed the scenery for a few minutes, then headed back to the car.

Usually, I like driving on these twisty roads, but Dov wanted to drive. So, I handed over the keys and away we went. On a few curves, it was pretty scary and I was hoping to have back at the wheel, but I just adjusted my seat and didn't say much. Driving for about an hour plus, and quite a few miles later, there was no sighting of elk, not even a shadow of one. Then, suddenly, right in the middle of the road up ahead, were four elk. Young ones with no rack, but who cares? They were elk.

Dov was bearing down on them, oblivious to what was in front of him. I grabbed his arm and shouted, "HEY, STOP!" Not sure if he had seen the elk, or if he would have just plowed right through them. We stop maybe 10 feet in front of them. Just like deer caught in headlights, except these were elk. I slowly raise my camera, moving ever so slightly not to spook them, and then, you won't believe what happened.

Dov blows the horn and the elk take off, faster than lightning.

I yelled, "WHY IN THE WORLD WOULD YOU DO A THING LIKE THAT? I WANTED TO TAKE A PICTURE!"

And what did Dov reply with? "OH, I didn't know you wanted to take a picture. I thought you just wanted to see them."

That was the last opportunity we had, as it got dark, and we never saw another elk.

# Chapter Twenty Two

## The Wisconsin Dells Trip

So much happened on this trip, it took me a while to recover. But, as you know, not often do you come back from a vacation refreshed and rested.

I guess the thing that sticks out the most in my mind about this trip is the kind people we met. Even though America has a lot of problems, it still is a great country with great people. Where else can you find strangers who are there when you need help, strangers who give you chocolate bars, strangers who walk you to the hotel office and explain what's in town, strangers with a smile greeting you, strangers willing to work on your car without asking, strangers who get in your car and drive you to the parts store? That's what sticks in my mind the most: the people we met. And, really, these people weren't strangers at all, only friends I hadn't met yet.

So, there we were, outside of Gary, Indiana, heading towards Wisconsin, on a toll road in a nasty traffic jam, go 10 feet, stop for while, 10 more feet and stop. Out of nowhere, this car pulls up with two girls, one waving a chocolate bar at us. Of course, I lean out the window to grab it. And it wasn't just any chocolate bar: it was a Macadamia Kona Coffee dark chocolate bar. Boy, was it good. Rich, in turn, grabbed a Little Debbie snack cake and said, "Here, give her this." It was a sight to see, stuck in traffic, exchanging snacks. We had a brief chat while our cars were parked. The girl that handed us the chocolate bar was from Vegas and in the Roller Derby.

About two hours or so later, somewhere in Illinois, not sure where because I dozed off, I awake in time to see us pass a gas station, only to run out of gas a short distance later. Rich had a habit of passing things on this trip, besides the gas station...like toll roads. He zipped through the gates without paying because he didn't know he had to stop. Anyway...Rich and Dov were trying to figure out what to do, when I stepped in and said, "Rich, come with me. We're going to walk to the nearest house and ask for a gas can." Simple solution!

We walked to a subdivision not far from the car. I told Rich, "This is no good. No one cuts their grass here, so, let's walk a bit further." He said, "No way. I'm going back." I continued on to the next house, and asked, "Do you have a gas can?" The guy said, "Sure. I'll help. Let me get a can and I'll drive you back." I got in his SUV and, in the quarter mile ride to the car, I knew how long Tim had lived in his house, what kind of dog he had, and how he switched professions. Tim drove us to the gas station and waited 'til we emptied the can and started up. He even let us keep the gas container. What a friendly gentleman. He was a real Godsend, so much so that I'm glad we ran out of gas; otherwise, we would never have met him.

Before I continue writing about the trip, I want to write about some of the other people we met. There was 12-year-old Timmy (yes, another Tim), from upper Wisconsin, that I met in the hotel parking lot. He showed me to the hotel office and informed me of places to eat and see in the Dells. He even wrote me weeks later to say "Hi." Also, there was Casha, the cute, witty Polish girl. And, we will never forget our friends at Stuff's Restaurant, a quaint little diner, complete with a mini bar. That was some breakfast at Stuff's. I guess it must have been the fresh Wisconsin air, lack of sleep, my observation of the place, reading about head cheese, or maybe all four that made me go into a silly comedy routine. I think it started when the waitress mentioned they had T-shirts for sale that said "Get Stuffed." I asked, "Would you happen to have underwear that said that?"

Dov and I talked Rich into buying a shirt, though he may have, anyways. I said, "Listen, you have to buy a shirt. I will take your photo, send it back to them, they will hang your picture on the wall, and you will be famous!" After taking a few photos of Rich, the waitress said, "Don't put the camera away - the chef's coming out in his attire." I answered, "He's coming out with a tire?" "NO, he's coming out fully-dressed in his chef's uniform." I replied back, "OH, I thought he was coming out with a tire to wheel us out." The whole place was laughing then. OK, so there were only 10 in the diner but, still, it was the whole place. When the photo shoot of Rich and the chef was over, I handed out my card and left. What fun!

Later on that day, in the hotel parking lot, I told Rich to open the hood of his car, so I could find out why the idle was so bad. Parked right next to us, looking under his hood, was a mechanic. When he heard Rich's car, he immediately said, "VACUUM LEAK." We didn't even ask him for help, but he came over and temporarily fixed the problem, until we could get to a dealer for the part.

Before taking off for Wisconsin, I called a trucker named Lee who lived there, whom I met at a Big Boy restaurant while he was on a run in Cleveland. He told me, "You have to go to a town named Baraboo and Devil's Lake." Taking his advice, we left the Dells, and on to Baraboo and Devil's Lake we went.

While in Baraboo, we stopped at an Oldsmobile dealer to buy the part for Rich's car. Fred, the owner, waited on us. They didn't have the part, but Fred said, "There is a Pontiac dealer outside of town that does, and I need to go there to pick up a car. How about if you drive me and I'll help you get the part?" Sure thing! Fred got in the back seat with me and I had the video camera on him until we arrived at the Pontiac dealer. He told us all about the area and stories about himself. His dad had bought the dealership in 1949.

One of the most interesting persons I met on the trip was the man at the bottom of the 14 steps of the Capitol building of Madison, Wisconsin. His name: OJ. His job: greeting people about to walk the last 14 steps to the observation deck, and answering questions they may have about the Capitol building, or anything else you care to ask.

We found out about Madison from Casha the Polish girl, who's here on a work visa. None of the locals told us about it. She said, "You have to go there. It's such a beautiful city, and surrounded by lakes." The two that surround the downtown area are Lake Mendota and Monona. Taking the main road into downtown, you can see a magnificent structure in the distance and, as you get closer, it gets even more impressive. That structure is the Capitol building.

We parked our car at a meter and, after a short walk through downtown Madison, Dov and Rich headed back to the car, bypassing the Capitol building. Not me. I had to investigate it and, boy, am I glad I did. All it took was one quick glance through the massive doors and I was completely wowed! I yelled at them to "Come on, the doors are open," but only Rich came. It was kind of funny watching Rich run in; maybe he was concerned with the meter, not sure. Have you ever seen one of those mazes where they let a mouse in, it scurries all over, finds the cheese, and heads out another opening? Well, that's what Rich looked like.

We walked in together, I went to the right, and he went to the left, and in a hurry. I stopped and watched him, thinking *We should be enjoying this together, but maybe he knows another way to the top floors.* Well, I got to the second level and still no Rich. So, I said to myself *Forget him*, and continued on alone, looking in doors and walking every floor. The Supreme Court room was something to behold. It made you feel like you had entered something sacred. You just have to see this building: the large badgers above the arches, the marble floors; even the doorknobs were engraved. The dome is the fourth largest in the world. The statue adorning the top of the dome is called Wisconsin, and the figures for her are equally impressive: the gilded bronze statue is 15 feet tall and weighs over three tons!

OJ filled me in on all this and more. He is an avid collector of old gas station memorabilia, and has traveled the fabled Route 66 and other routes, in search of merchandise, photos and information about them.

After about a 20-minute-or-more talk with OJ, I left to find Rich and Dov. They both angrily jumped at me. I said, "Hey, I met this fascinating guy and did you see the Supreme Court Room? The Observation Deck?" Rich replied, "No, I went in, saw what I wanted, took a few photos and left, and what did I tell you, Dov, why Carey was taking so long? He met someone." Of course I did. Did they expect me not to?

Maybe Rich was justified in being mad; I know I was gone a LONG time, long enough where they ate lunch, so maybe it was an hour and twenty minutes, not twenty, but, then again, I can't tell time.

OK! I wrote about the people we met, and now, I will tell you my perspective on Wisconsin and the Dells.

Compared to the scenery in other states I've been to, the area we drove through and surrounding the Dells was quite disappointing. I had heard about the Dells and seen it in old travel brochures, but it just didn't live up to my expectations. What I had envisioned was more natural, a gorge-type river, something in the way of the Genesee River in Letchworth State Park, New York, but surrounded by tourist shops that blended in. This was definitely not the case.

In fact, besides a few areas and the boat ride we took, it was hard to find a good view of the Wisconsin River or Lake Delton. We had to drive away from the Dells to get an open view of the Wisconsin River. That's how much the Dells are built up!

Even on the boat ride, the scenery, rock formations and sandstone were very beautiful and can only be found in one other place in the world. But, still, it wasn't as spectacular as I thought it would be, unless we took the wrong boat ride and there was more to see. One thing that got my attention was the dark brown water. It's not dirty, but from tannin, which tea contains.

I was also surprised by the lack of cheese stores and other specialty shops usually found in places rooted in the German culture. I thought the Dells would play up on that theme, as in Frankenmuth, Michigan. Wisconsin is a big state, so maybe there are other areas where they do.

BUT, if you're into water parks and amusement-type atmosphere, with little trinket shops, it's an excellent place to vacation. The Dells is billed as "The Water Park Capital of the World" and has America's largest water park, Noah's Ark. It seemed like a strange setting for all those water parks and I couldn't figure out the tie-in with the area; they seemed misplaced. We chose not to go to any but, instead, browsed the shops, went sightseeing and people watched.

Outside of the Dells, the scenery changed for the better. Not far from Baraboo, which is a neat little city, was Devil's Lake. The name "Devil's Lake" was mis-translated from the Indians. American Indians actually called it Spirit Lake. The water was so sparkling clean, it was incredible. You could see right to the bottom, with a clear view of all the pebbles and rocks.

We concluded the trip at Madison, the capital of Wisconsin. As I mentioned, I found that city to be beautiful.

# Chapter Twenty Three

## Notes from Texas –
## Lake Summerville Hydrocross

The way Walt drove, it was as if he was qualifying early for the jet ski race. Twenty four hours to get here from Cleveland; left Thursday 1:30 a.m., stopped about 6:30 a.m. for three hours, to sleep in the truck at a roadside rest. I opted for better sleeping quarters, so I slept on a picnic table. Not bad until the cleaning lady woke me with her sweeping.

Drove till Friday 2:00 a.m., grabbed six hours sleep at a motel. Arrived at Lake Somerville, 104 degrees and sunny.

I haven't seen all of Texas but, what I have seen, I was just not that impressed with the scenery. The land was flat and, for the most part, brown.

It cooled down today: only 98. I spoke with a lady on Saturday and she said this was their 32$^{nd}$ day in triple digits, which is abnormal. I asked, "How hot does it usually get?" She said, "99!"

I was equally amused by the six-day weather forecast. It read 95 - 94 - 96 - **98 HOT** - 96 - 95. "98 Hot?" What is 95 and 96, a cold front?

The day of the jet ski race it was HOT – whether out of the water or in the water! Walt took two second-place victories in his class, not bad for the first time racing jet skis.

Two things I didn't see down here were liberals and vegans. They're probably somewhere in Texas, but not the area I was in. A vegan would starve here; almost all the diners, restaurants and bars have in big letters either STEAKS or BARBEQUE. But, they do serve a vegetable with your dinner.

What I did see was quite a few monuments with "In God We Trust." San Antonio was named after the Catholic Saint San Antonio de Padua.

San Antonio was very impressive and, to me, it's a hidden gem. Unless I have been out of the loop, I just don't remember hearing much talk about it being a travel destination. I loved the river walk and all the historic sites and the tacky tourist shops alongside better gift shops. It was confusing, though; with all the Mexican-made gifts and logos, it was hard to tell what country I was in.

The Alamo – now, that was surprising! I always pictured it out in the middle of some barren desert, all alone. But, in fact, it's right in the middle of San Antonio. It was closed when we got there, but I was able to look in through the iron gate. Impressive!

Directly across the Alamo is a monument honouring the dead who tried to defend the fort. Jim Bowie and Davy Crockett were among the names listed. A few teenagers were running up this monument to have their photos taken. Sitting on a bench directly in front of it was an old man. He looked homeless. Of course, I had to talk with him. His name was Jonathan. I wish I had more time to sit there and converse with him, but my group was heading to the Guinness Museum. In the short time I did have, Jonathan told me his family has been in America for 300 years. He was very upset and angry at those teens that were running all over the monument and disrespecting the men who gave their lives. Jonathon said, "If they only understood how hallowed this ground is."

Here was a man who appeared homeless, and what was he complaining about? Not his situation, but the lack of respect being shown to the heroes of this nation. That's the true American spirit.

In all, it was a fun and memorable trip.

# Chapter Twenty Four

## Anything to See

I posted on Craigslist a well-built, old dresser. A lady responded from Norwalk, Ohio, which is about 80 miles and an hour and a half away from my house. She asked if I would deliver it to her. Of course I said "Yes."

I drive out there and, after I unload the dresser and put it in her house, I asked, "Is there anything to see around here?" She said, "Well, I can show you my old dishes."

She opened the door on her hutch and, sure enough, she showed me her dishes. I didn't know what else to say, other than "Those are really nice. I need to head out now. Thanks for showing them to me!"

# Chapter Twenty Five

## The Factory of Terror

This is my recount of the night I spent in the Factory of Terror, or better known as the old Hercules Engine plant in Canton, Ohio.

Psychic Sonya and I arrived at the abandoned factory about 1:00 a.m. on Saturday or, to us third-shifters, late Friday night. We met up with a second group that had just started lining up. The tour to spend a night in the factory was a promotion for radio station 92Q in Alliance, Ohio. Sonya knew the DJ at 92Q and also the owners of the building. So, she was allowed to bring a few guests. The rest on the tour were contestant winners. We freely roamed about the place 'til about a little after 5:00 a.m.

So, what was my impression of spending a night in a supposedly haunted factory? Did I see anything? Did people freak? Would I do it again? Of course I would. There's nothing like a spine-tingling chill to awaken your senses, but maybe you should spend the night and find out for yourself what it's like.

Being honest, though, I actually didn't experience a feeling of being spooked as much as a feeling of sadness and gloom. Here was a factory that once employed thousands, now in decay and empty. It was very eerie walking around this place. My mind wandered more on what it was like in the early days during the Civil War, when the factory was built, who worked here, was it mostly Poles, Germans or mixed?

I thought about the excitement in Canton, as the factory kept growing. The men who made a good living to support their families, the husband running home to tell his wife his raise came through. The increased activity through all the wars: the Civil War, WWI, WWII, Korean, Vietnam, and possibly even Desert Storm. With all the changes through the years inside the factory and outside, it kept growing and expanding. It changed hands twice, and returned back to the original company. Then, suddenly, the doors were slammed shut for good, no warning, just "Pack your stuff and leave - the factory is closing." That's where my mind wandered and wondered.

As we walked from room to room, I noticed the changes through the years, as new sections were added. In the building constructed during the Civil War, it was more massive. The original timbers are still there, supporting the ceiling, all in good shape. The stone walls showed the marks of the chisel used to shape them. Very impressive! In the newer sections it is more utilitarian, with less workmanship, less character - just an old run-down building.

Within the boiler room there was another small room that was hard to reach, with a low sloping ceiling. It had a desk and locker with supplies for the maintenance man. It was here that workers escaped to take a nap and goof off. I learned this from a lady who was on the tour with us. She said her father used to work at the engine plant.

In another area of the factory was a workstation and shelving area that housed a collection of Stroh's beer and liquor bottles. All seemed to be from the same time period: the late 50s to early 60s. As I was snooping around, I noticed the bottles hidden under the shelves. I wondered, *Why all the same bottles? How did they survive all these years in the same place? Why didn't anyone notice them before and not throw them out? Were they all consumed by the same guy? Was he the factory drunk? Was he fired, and that's why the bottles were from the same years?* Just makes one wonder.

In another area we found forklifts, all lined up in a row. It seemed they were parked as they normally would for the next shift, but the next shift never came. There they sat, never to be used again. One large room had the engines. Some were still in crates, others in parts, and one was their showpiece, polished and never meant to be sold. This engine showcased their pride in workmanship.

Twenty-eight acres in the middle of Canton - 10 acres of building, all connected - now mostly empty and decaying. How sad!

As I wrote, I didn't really feel anything spooky or supernatural. I usually don't get frightened of these things, anyways. I am more concerned with the natural of who could possibly be in this place. The owner of the building also shared the same opinion. He has to walk around at night, making sure all the doors are secure and he's always worried about a homeless person sneaking in and robbing him. With a group as large as ours, I wasn't a bit worried about that happening.

BUT, the supernatural does exist - it is real! Before I headed out to the factory, a few friends asked why I would get involved with something like this. My answer is simple: I'm quite knowledgeable about the supernatural and know how to handle it. But, I would never recommend this to someone who is skittish or has fears. You really shouldn't attempt to dabble into the supernatural. It can open doors in your life that can haunt you for years. Trust me on this.

While in the ice house, which was an old part of the building temporarily used as a morgue during a cholera outbreak in the 1800s, Sonya had a strange experience. She said she felt someone brush up against her and heard a little girl's voice whispered to her, "I'm cold." Sonya had visited this old place several times in the past, and she said this wasn't the first time she had an unusual experience in this part of factory.

Another person in our group kept complaining that her flashlight was going on and off by itself. And, when

we entered a different room, this same person complain-
ed loudly that someone hit her in the head. She said she
felt like she had been hit with a rock. It was definitely
not any of us, as most of the group was very stiff and
fearful. Some of them were so spooked and serious, they
didn't even laugh when I said I found Jimmy Hoffa, or
that maybe Geraldo Rivera could do a special on the
place, like he did with Al Capone's Vault.

As for myself, I was more adventurous, and took off
into the small back section of the boiler room,
rummaging through all the books and catalogs. I was in
there for quite a while. The group started calling for me,
but I ignored their first two calls. Then I heard the
concern in their voices: "Are you OK?" So, I gave up on
the rummaging and rejoined the group.

I did get a little scared, though, when I dropped back
from everyone on purpose to do my own investigating.
All I had with me was a little penlight - that's it! Hey, if
you're going to roam a place at night, you might as well
do it right. What fun would it be with a bright flashlight?

Anyway, this place is like a maze. I went through the
cafeteria and that opened into three different hallways.
With three ways to go, I chose hall number two. Went
down that and it came to three more doors. Opened one,
and it led to a small, dark alley outside that was spooky,
not knowing if someone was lurking out there. So,
before freaking, I gathered myself and realized the other
doors weren't it either; I had the wrong hallway. How

did I know it without opening them? The spider webs weren't disturbed. So, I turned around and found my way back.

Did I capture anything on film? YES! The photo I took of the windows shows one with an orb and one without. I took two shots of the same window to make sure it came out, not because I saw the orb in person, but because glass can sometimes reflect and ruin a photo. The other orb I caught was when I crawled up into the chimney. In another, there was a white ball. Was it an orb or a reflection of something? If the images were caused by spots on the lens, they would be in all the photos.

The most eerie photo is a picture with a… You know what? I will leave you guessing; maybe you will have the opportunity to experience the Haunted Factory yourself and will find what I saw. Or, maybe it will find you first!

In all, it was a very intriguing fun-filled night.

BOO!

# Chapter Twenty Six

## That's Old

I attended Mr. Rudd's auction in Blue Creek, Ohio. Mr. Rudd had a Christmas light display on his property. The display had over a million lights on 50 acres. He was having health issues and was planning to retire. It was just too much for him to handle. Everything had to go.

His grandson, who was maybe about seven at that time, had taken to me, which I didn't mind at all. We took a walk around the property; all the while, the grandson was explaining to me what the barns and stables were used for, what kinds of animals Grandpa kept, what his grandpa stored in the shed, and other interesting facts about the Christmas Farm that I gladly listened to and enjoyed.

We walked to the edge of Mr. Rudd's property, where an old - I mean old - barn stood. This old, weathered barn had to be easily over a hundred years old. So, I asked the grandson, "That's an old barn - how old is it?" Shaking his head, he slowly answered, "I don't know; it's old. It's been here since I was a kid."

# Chapter Twenty Seven

## Road to a Friend's House

It was so good to get away from everything, and I mean everything. Away from politics, TV, toilet, shower – OK, maybe not those last two, but it was good to get away.

Millard lives out in a holler, as he calls it, or the boonies, as I call it. Thank goodness I've been blessed with a built-in homing device; otherwise, I never would have found his place at night.

The directions he wrote to his house read like this: *Turn on hwy 520. By grocery store. Go to Top of Hill.* OK, right away, I was confused: "Top of Hill?" Almost the entire state of Kentucky is a hill or mountain. *Turn left sign says "E Mountain." Then go several miles till get to rock with a gate sitting by it.*

Rock? Did he write ROCK? He failed to mention the road to his place is lined with monolithic, giant rocks. I mean, these aren't your ordinary city rocks that line driveways; these are more like huge stonewalls. And gate? Do you know how hard it is driving around hairpin curves in total darkness on roads barely wide enough for two cars, looking for a gate?

Where were we...? *...till get to rock with a gate sitting by it. Turn their. their are two green signs one says "Lost Hills Rd" (no kidding!) other sign says "Oak Rd" turn at "Lost Hills Rd" sign. Go till see brown trailer on a hill.*

I don't think I have to point out how hard it is to find a brown trailer at night, do I?

*There will be a camper their. There will be a white car parked at bottom of hill next to a hog pen. Theirs no hog in pen. They killed one for pig roast. Killed other two and put in freezer. Gave us some meat.*

(Yes, that was EXACTLY how he wrote it!)

Do you see what a nighttime driving adventure this was? How's a city boy supposed to know the difference between a hog pen from any other kind of pen, especially at night? A pen is a pen, unless you mean the state pen; now that, I understand. But, good thing he mentioned there were no hogs in the pen. That helped out loads, as I did find his place.

I don't get spooked easily, but it was a bit unnerving walking up to a trailer at night, no one around, no lights on, not knowing if I had the correct trailer. In these parts, the first thing you're liable to hear before they ask what you want is BANG! But, someone had to find out and, since I was alone, I had to send myself. Thank God I was at the right place and a friendly face opened the door.

# Personal Note!

I included this because it shows a much simpler way of thinking and lifestyle than what we are used to in the city, not to make fun.

And I must add...

DO NOT attempt to follow these directions in search of his house. I changed the names of the roads to protect his privacy. If you do find a Rt. 520 or a large rock with a gate by it and a brown trailer, it's probably the wrong one but, if you're brave enough, go ahead and knock anyways.

# Chapter Twenty Eight

## Thank God for Teachers

I was in southern Ohio, around the Hillsboro area. Surfing the radio while driving, I came across a preacher with a heavy Southern accent.

I just love Southern preachers. Whether Baptist or Pentecostal, their fiery passion for the Gospel is so sincere, it just moves you.

This particular radio preacher was on the topic of thanking God for everything. He went on and on, naming just about everything under the sun you should thank God for.

He then mentioned teachers: "Even teachers...you need to be thankful. Without them, you wouldn't know anything because they are the ones who learned you how to write, they learned you English, they learned you math, they learned you history..."

# Chapter Twenty Nine

## The Sandy Lake Supper

Ruth, my niece Tiffiny, and I stopped in Sandy Lake, PA. Earlier in the day, we were in Mesopotamia, Ohio, enjoying their Ox Roast and Flea Market, held every July 4th weekend, a terrific event that's recommended. I got the brilliant idea at 4:00 p.m. to drive to Tionesta, PA., about a hundred miles away. That's why we stopped in Sandy Lake. It was the halfway point and it was getting late; we needed to eat. Tionesta would have to wait for another day.

We located Sandy Lake's local grocery store to pick up what we needed for grilling our supper. When I pulled into the lot, a lady came running out to ask, "What is this thing you're driving?" I told her, "Why, this is the Go-Go Bus." Ruth and Tiffiny were beyond hungry and wanted nothing to do with this chitchat. They were even more upset when I followed the lady into her health food store. Well, I had to. I felt obligated when the lady said, "I am closed, but will open it back up just for you." I bought a few potatoes and left. Later, Ruth and Tiffiny insisted the lady came out wearing a bra and thought I was nuts for going with her. I wasn't so sure it was a bra. I thought it was just a skimpy top. Then again, maybe it was a bra; but, honest, I didn't follow her for that reason.

We finished our shopping and started our search for a picnic site. Right outside of the grocery store, just a short walk away, was their city park. Definitely an odd setting, shoehorned between side streets, behind the post office and grocery store. And, if you pulled in the wrong drive, you ended up in the adjacent factory. The park had a pavilion, a swing set, two grills, maybe four trees, and that's it. Ruth and Tiffiny wanted to eat there, but I wasn't content. I wanted to find a place to eat within Goddard State Park, by the lake. I won, so off we went.

After a little bit of driving and searching, I found a perfect spot close to the lake. Just beautiful! A family had reserved the only pavilion, but I asked if they minded if we join them. The reply was, "Not at all." We unloaded our things while overhead clouds started moving in rapidly. Lightning started to flash, but we were undaunted. We were going to eat. I didn't have any paper to start the fire, so I told Ruth, "Use the map. I don't need it." That decision would come back to haunt me.

The three of us were busy like beavers, cutting up meat, chopping potatoes, with Ruth trying to start a fire. Then, suddenly, the heavens opened up a deluge on us. I mean opened up, monsoon-like. A family of bicyclists darted in and took refuge under the shelter to wait it out. It didn't last too long, but everything got wet. Boy, oh boy, did I hear it from Ruth and Tiffiny: "Now what are we going to do?" "I am hungry." "I have a headache..." I just took it in stride the best I could. We threw everything back into the Go-Go Bus, which was now in complete disarray, and we headed out in search of a dryer setting.

I drove to another shelter I spotted while driving but, it turned out it was part of a church, not a park, so plan C: back to the town of Sandy Lake and their community park. It actually turned out to be perfect; obviously, not as scenic, but the pavilion was shaped like a Nipa Hut, which made Ruth happy. It was dry, which meant we could eat; that made Tiffiny happy, and it had electricity, which made me happy because I could plug in my hot plate to start cooking and quiet the restless natives that were about to hang me. But, the biggest blessing was the wood. Right across the street was an empty house. It had a large pile of dried, broken branches. I had all the firewood I needed to cook.

The supper was delicious: chicken wings, western-style pork ribs, corn on the cob, spinach and sliced potatoes, fried. All that angst for nothing! Actually, though, it got a little worse when I got lost and added hours to our trip home. Remember that map I told Ruth to use to start the fire because I didn't need it? Well, I needed it.

100

# Chapter Thirty

## We started this book with breakfast so now let's end it with...

## A BANG!

We had just finished our supper in the City Park of Sandy Lake, and started to load up our cookware and gear. There was stillness to the air, after the earlier thunderstorm. The temperature had moderated and all was quiet. The time was approximately 8:20 p.m. when a BOOM shattered the silence. I don't get startled too often, but this frightened me. It was one of the scariest noises I have ever heard.

The boom seemed like it lasted a good three seconds, maybe more. It shook the ground; that's how powerful it was. The sound reverberated over the foothills of the Alleghenies; then, there was a repercussion, as it bounced back and made another boom, though much lower in sound and power.

Tiffiny was as spooked as Ruth and I were, and said, "Let's get out of here." I was temporarily speechless. We waited and thought for sure we would hear sirens wailing or some warning, but nothing came. Ruth, who is from the Philippines, said she has heard bombs before, and this was no explosion or fireworks; it definitely sounded like a bomb.

We finished packing and, heading out, we drove past the volunteer fire department. A group of people were standing outside talking. I asked if they heard the explosion. They just smiled. I said, "I know this is still the 4th of July weekend, but this was no firework." Again, they just smiled.

I tried to come up with an explanation for what we heard, but they didn't make much sense. I thought, *Could it be a fracking accident? Dynamite being used in a coal mine?* I searched online, but never saw a report or news story about this incident.

What was that Sandy Lake BOOM? It remains a mystery!

# In Closing

Hey Gang,

Hope you enjoyed this!

If you did, you may be wondering if another book is in the works. Well... as long as there are people to meet and places to see, I will always have a story waiting to be told, so it's quite possible.

Who knows? Maybe I will meet you on the road and a new friendship and adventure could begin, and that could be the start of book number two.

If you would like to keep abreast of my latest travels go to my website at www.GoGobus.cc.

Until then....
Gotta Go-Go!
Carey Masci

43210423R00066

Made in the USA
Lexington, KY
21 July 2015